All That Shines

Under The Hollywood Sign

Iris Berry

Punk ★ Hostage ★ Press

All That Shines
Under The Hollywood Sign

Introduction
Joe Donnelly

Editor
Michele McDannold

Cover & Illustrations
Scott Aicher

Original photograph of Oki Dog by Edward Colver
Original photograph of the L.A. River by Kevin Break

Punk Hostage Press
Hollywood, USA
www.punkhostagepress.com

For A. Razor

And

Lee McGrevin,
'May he rest in peace'

Introduction

Iris Berry is one of my true literary loves.

I love her like I love the city that articulates through her words. This is the kind of love you don't know you've been looking for until you find it. Then, there it is one day, where it's always been, under your nose, though you had failed to apprehend it all these years because, like this city, there is so much you don't see until you finally do.

When I met Iris, she was blond, gap-toothed, bruised and bomb shelled, like a hotrod Lauren Hutton. Though, given her quick quips and hard boil, maybe I really mean Bacall. To many, she was already the stuff of legend—of Disgraceland, of Ringling Sisters, of microphones and whispers—a gun moll and getaway driver. But, I was lucky enough to have arrived after the din had died down a bit and the legend could become fact over lunches shared in cracked vinyl booths at a long-gone diner under a shadow where the slow dawn meets new and different days in the places where we used to walk and talk, but don't anymore.

We'd take our time in there because the leafy streets were a couple blocks away and it was too bright outside. Inside, though, it was just right with the A/C and the Reuben sandwiches, thick fries and the coffees and cookies. Friends and acquaintances—some writers, some musicians, some lovers, many neighbors—would come and go and say hello.

In those cracked booths, Iris would fortify me with her commitment to herself and to her work, to the home and homesickness that is her muse. She wrote and when I read what she wrote, I felt closer to a place we'd traveled far to get to, but maybe hadn't yet arrived at, and maybe never would.

Such is the lot of the writer.

Before long, I came to know there was no dichotomy. Iris was exactly the Los Angeles I'd been seeking all this time, a place where legend and truth were neither paradoxical nor oppositional. Instead, they were the shadow and light with which she wrote the folklore of these ephemeral days, giving our legends and truths a place that feels like home, at last.

In her hands, *The Daughters of Bastards* find refuge from their wrecked childhoods in the rubble of Hollywood and the voices echoing throughout *Two Blocks East of Vine* grow raspy in their resilience and the flotsam of *All That Shines Under the Hollywood Sign* may be forsaken, but it won't be forgotten.

They say her city is disappearing, that there is less room for legend and truth now; that we have to have one or the other. I don't believe it. Without our folklore, we could be anywhere, and if we could be anywhere, we are probably lost. But if you're holding this book, you're not. You are walking and talking with Iris under the Hollywood sign.

Let it shine.

~ Joe Donnelly
Visiting Assistant Professor of English and Journalism, Whittier College, Author of the collection *L.A. Man: Profiles from a Big City and a Small World.*

Thank you...

To my mom & dad (r.i.p.) for moving the family
out west, way back when, and for so much more. My three
brothers: Don, Paul & Marty. And my nephew Jake.

Razor & all the writers at Punk Hostage Press.
Michele McDannold, Joe Donnelly, Scott Aicher,
Richard Modiano & everyone at Beyond Baroque Literary
Arts Center, Red Stodolsky & Baroque Books,

Dave Alvin, Pleasant Gehman, Judy Farrell, S.A. Griffin,
Keith Morris, Amanda Toland, Susan Hayden, Vicky
Hamilton, Puma Perl, Teddy Quinn, Marina Lenter, Chris
Bailey, Sam McBride, Nadia Bruce Rawlings, Gwenn
Morreale, Vivien Cooper, Shane Enholm, Mickey McMahan
for "Henry Mancini", Dimitri Monroe for Everything,
Maxine Brummer & Jenna James aka the sisters of the Sun
Room. Violet Liquori, Nicholas Berry, and Lola, Elton &
Puss...

Contents

Those who can afford it
don't understand it
those who understand it
can't afford it…

~ Robert Manuel Jacobson

Standing directly
in front of the Hollywood Sign,
I can feel its majestic pull.
All nine letters, each one 45 feet tall
and 30 feet wide.
Built in 1923, an 18-month ad campaign
that's lasted 96 years and counting.
It's taken on a life of its own
promising many things to many people.
All I've ever wanted from it
is to just sit there and look good,
and it's never let me down...

Thank You, Henry Mancini

Thank you

Henry Mancini

for all the neon boulevards

and all the city streets

of all the cities

and the jazz

and the poetry

of the downtowns

and the uptowns.

For Sunset Boulevard

in the rain

Hollywood Boulevard

at twilight

and Wilshire Boulevard

at dawn.

For the Pacific Coast Highway

Union Station

and the view

from Mulholland Drive

both sides

the San Fernando Valley

and Los Angeles.

For jazz gliding its way

down translucent highways

at one in the morning

through the steam

of car headlights

in the pouring rain.

For making me feel clean

when I was dirty

and for the fantasy

that my life

was somehow better

than it was

and for the romance

when there wasn't any.

For crazy but surprisingly

smooth hung-over mornings

when an all-nighter

should have been painful.

Thank you

for the lengthy

warm

Santa Ana

summer afternoons

overlooking a city

from a dingy apartment

with only the view

and you

to save me.

Thank you

Henry Mancini

for those

ephemeral evenings

draped across Hollywood

at midnight

like a ghost town

timeless

glamorous

and still.

For the exquisite

and the calm

and for the clean

and regal lift of elegance

onto a stairway of stars

leading to a luxurious

and illustrious world

where nothing earthly

can touch me

thank you.

In the Shadow of The Hollywood Sign

(*Excerpt from the Pink Mansion - The Daughters of Bastards*)

In 1982

the streets of Hollywood

were vacant and barren,

a ghost town,

like the abandoned movie

set that it was.

No tourists, no glamour.

Just a has-been stretch of a boulevard

with tarnished and littered stars

on a sidewalk of Babylon dreams.

Inhabited by homeless

leftover Hollywood hopefuls,

pushing shopping carts,

talking about Frank Sinatra and Lana Turner,

still waiting to get discovered.

And a bunch of us punk rock kids

from broken homes,

or no homes,

trying to figure it all out,

running wild in the abandoned streets

and having the time of our lives.

It felt very pre-apocalyptic.

We were all waiting

for the world to end in 1984.

With two years left to go,

there was no time to waste.

The world did end in 1984,

but not in the way Orwell predicted,

he was a few decades off.

It ended for us in Los Angeles

by having the 1984 Olympics here.

People from all over the world

attended the festivities

and realized all the opportunity,

a whole new kind of gold rush.

They came back

and turned Los Angeles

into a city that I

no longer recognize…

no longer the city

where I could feel

the celebrated spirits

of so many Eras.

The 1970s and the politically,

rebellious, rock n roll 1960s

on the Sunset Strip,

or the glamour and corruption

of the 1950s,

and the roar of the 'New Hollywood'

in the 1920s

on Hollywood Boulevard.

Even though Hollywood was abandoned in 1982,

there were still left-over remnants

from the celebrations.

All the old ghosts

and some of the old haunts were still here.

And I was in love with it all...

The Garden of Allah

Flappers and flasks

flaunting mint-juleps

in the South of France.

Expatriates and intellects.

Hemingway's tales of manhood.

F. Scott and Zelda

in love.

Algonquin late nights

and New York Socialites

sipping Gin Rickeys

Benchley's so witty

Parker's suicides

Zelda's insanity

and F. Scott's success.

The movie-boom

came too soon

Hollywood's Golden Years

talking pictures

end careers

soon read the headlines:

"DEATH FROM THE HOLLYWOOD SIGN."

Slow death from the bottle

a broken F. Scott

talk of the town

riding drunk

on the hood of cars

causing scenes

in all the bars

<u>fee</u>ding the hungry press.

26

And Zelda more and more

becoming less and less

everyone drinking and drinking

till the fruits of love

rotted in the Garden of Allah

with Madame Nazimova,

Bogart and Baby,

Orson and Lilly,

Sheila Graham and a finished F. Scott.

Till there was no more garden

till there was no more F. Scott.

And as Zelda lay down

in with the sleep

came the fire

till there was

no more Zelda.

All That Shines Under the Hollywood Sign

Being a native Angeleno
no matter where I've gone
and where I go,
Pacoima,
Encino
or San Marino?
Hollywood looms large

and its reach
is long and powerful
the names
of famous streets
are forever imprinted
into my memory bank.
Seeing them
in my everyday life
on TV
in the movies
and hearing their names
in songs.

Topanga Canyon,
Laurel Canyon,
Van Nuys Boulevard,
Hollywood and Vine,
Sunset and Vine,
the Sunset Strip,
and Mullholland Drive.

People come here
from all over the world
knowing the names
of these streets and boulevards.
Taking the 101 freeway
and seeing those famous

street names on off ramps
is like a visual roll call
where each one of the street names
could have their own IMDB page.

When I was 16
and I'd cut school
instead of running off
with my friends
to get high
in their parent's garage
I'd take a drive to Venice Beach
leisurely and without traffic
if I didn't take Topanga Canyon
I'd go through Hollywood,
take the Sunset Strip
all the way to PCH
and find my way
to the Venice boardwalk
when it was still soaked
with the perfect blend of
the 1950s Beat era
and 1960s and 70s hippy cultures
with a big dose
of Bob Dylan
and Jim Morrison.
I met some of the most talented people

performing on that Boardwalk.
But before I'd hit the beach
I'd stop off
at Schwab's Drugstore
on the corner of
Sunset Boulevard and Laurel Canyon
buy myself some breakfast
with a front row seat
at the counter
watching all the actors,
musicians,
and all kinds of characters
come and go
and most of them
would find a way
to talk to me.
I was young
and bright eyed
with a purse full of
stolen red lipstick
from the make-up counter.
Some of them
offered to discover me
some of them
wanted to *keep* me.
This was a time before
milk cartons

—

the internet
and investigative television
but I still knew better.

Schwab's is gone now
along with so many other
Hollywood landmarks
and even though
I was only 16
I knew at the time
how incredible it was.
So, before I'd leave Schwab's
for the beach
I'd make a stop
at those regal
wood phonebooths
in the back.
I'd close the door
and the light would come on
and I'd call my brother
and I'd say to him,
"guess where I am…"

The Trouble with Palm Trees

Part #1

Palm trees
standing gorgeous
erect and regal
they call to me
they whisper things
to each other
they glisten in the hot
California sun
they promise
many things
to many people
fame
fortune
love
sweet summer romance…
somehow
all I ever got from them
is they're nice
to look at
and they've never
failed me.

The Trouble with Palm Trees

Part #2

The problem
with palm trees is
there's nothing
practical about them
they offer no shade
in the summer
and no warmth
in the winter
they just
look good
how perfect
for California.

L.A. River Lullaby

It's 2:06 am
I can hear the sounds
of a distant train
as the constant passing of cars
drive the 5 freeway
alongside the L.A. River
heading north
and heading south
going to places called home.
Home for me

is not a place

with walls

windows and doors

where framed photographs

are placed on mantles

over fireplaces

and lined hallways

or embedded

in refrigerator magnets.

Home lives in my heart

and in my breath

and in the unsaid exchange

of knowing glimpses

with loved ones

and kindred spirits

ignited by

the reciprocity

of trust

kindness

safety

love

and the generosity

of a spirit

that goes beyond

material items.

Beyond

coaxing words

and gestures

for planned outcomes

beyond any exchange

of anything

wanted

or needed.

Home is not

the room

for the life

but for the life

in the room.

Home lives

in the conversations

that our souls

are having

with each other

without words

where truths

are unspoken

with an unconditional love

that rings louder

and with more power

than mere words

could ever express

with an emanating

everlasting

unstoppable

force.

Home is anywhere

the heart thrives…

As the passing cars

on the 5 freeway

get quieter and quieter

until all I can hear

is the distant train

and the unspoken words.

Shooting for the Stars in Kevlar

We run

from hot summer days

and broken air conditioners

we run

to chilled movie theatres

make out like teenagers

who've never had sex

never been kissed

by tender mouths

and never cradled

in the arms

of an unconditional love.

We make

our own movies

back in the back

of the theatre

laughing like there's no yesterday

yesterdays that begged us to stay

and tried to kill us

in our sleep

then chased us

in our waking hours

begging for salvation

and a hall pass.

We are

the bright spots

in the road

found in

dark alleys.

A pair of lives

lived hard

treated hard

and discarded harder

and as we

hit the pavement

skipping

we forgot

that we were only

playing hopscotch

to the tune of songs

lead by a symphony

of sirens and howling dogs.

Can we believe

that we can believe in love?

After we have let so many

put their unloving hands

around our hearts

souls and throats

x-friends

x-loves

x-drug habits

x-drug dealers

still trying

to strike a better deal

with empty promises

empty pockets

and empty souls.

Leaving

open wounds

like bullets holes

as the winds blow

through them

hollow and scarred

and that sometimes

most often

are unhealable.

A catalog
of catastrophic events
shaped our lives
and sculpted us
into who we are.
It doesn't always mean
that who we are
can carry us
into who we want to be…
but that doesn't mean we'll stop trying.

As we
dry our eyes
while no one's looking
in dark theaters
waiting for the next
movie to start.

What Makes Eddie Run

(For Eddie Little rip)

I see you sitting

sitting in the glow

of your computer

burnt spoon and needle

at one side

and a loaded gun

at the other.

There's only one bullet

in the chamber

and it's reserved for you.

You're attempting to write

the next great American novel

and I believe you will

providing you don't kill yourself

before it's finished.

It's a race

isn't it?

your conscience

and your ego

are at a dead heat
while your phone
is ringing off the hook
with calls from your agent
and London and New York
all wanting to buy
the Movie rights.

You were the first guy
to ever buy me diamonds
I'm just wondering
where you got the money.
Was it an insurance scam?
Phony credit cards?
Or your usual
selling phony stocks
to old people
for their life savings?

Well, all I can say is
it's only a matter of time
for you sweetheart.
But if it's true
that nice guys and gals

finish last

then you can bet

I'll be sitting

in the last seat

in the last row

of the house

that I more than likely

bought at 100% mark-up

trapped between

a noisy bathroom

and a rank alley way.

But at least

while I'm sitting

on the lap of time

checking my watch

I know you'll be

mixing another shot

of liquid comfort

while running

from that god-awful mirror

called your conscience

there aren't enough opiates

in the city of L.A.

to make that reflection go away

but I know you

you're not a quitter

you'll die trying.

The Ghosts of Punk Rock Past

The First time we met

was on a Saturday night

in 1978 or '79.

He was running down

Sunset Boulevard

with about

five other people,

they were all covered in peanut butter.

He stopped right in front of me

and sweetly said,

"We're smearing peanut butter

all over ourselves,

you wanna do it with us?"

My friends were horrified

and pulled me away.

I was intrigued.

About a year later

we were in his apartment

on Cherimoya and Franklin

which was literally

in the shadow of the

Hollywood Sign.

There was about 10 kittens

running around

and bouncing off the walls,

it was a flying cat circus.

He liked to say my name backwards,

"Hey, Siri! Give me your arm?"

and before I knew it

he grabbed my wrist

and just as his

lit cigarette

was about to hit my skin

one of the kittens

flew into us

and knocked it

out of his hands.

The last time

I saw him

was at Oki Dog.

It was about 2:30

in the morning

he was walking around

saying goodbye

to people

one by one...

and the next day

just like that

he was gone.

Since then

there's been

so many others

and I think about it

these encounters

brief and fleeting

and otherwise.

These bonds

surreal and otherworldly

in life as in death.

These chance meetings.

And I don't know

what any of it means

I'm just glad

we met

along the way.

Christmas in Van Nuys at Ralph's Market at Midnight

The lights are cruel
at Ralph's Market
in Van Nuys at midnight.
Apparently, it's Christmas
according to the aisles
at Ralph's Market.
But if I had to guess
by the customers
I'd say it was Halloween.
It's desperate here in Ralph's
at midnight
and the lights don't help.
Florescent lights
are never good for the complexion.
There's a young homeless couple
walking the aisles buying food
and looking happy
at least they're in a relationship
I think to myself.
Freshly home from a trip

to *The Big Apple*

I went with my boyfriend

and came home single.

We had to go

3,000 miles to break up?

It happened

in bed

in the dark

at 3 in the morning

in a dingy

Times Square

hotel room.

It was epic

and when that

plane landed

20 hours later

on California soil

I clicked my heels

and quietly chanted

there's no place like home

there's no place like home

there's no place like home.

56

And now I am home
in my neighborhood
Ralph's Market
feeling like I don't belong.

The thing about California
with its constant sunshine
the only way to tell the seasons
is by what's selling on the shelves
at the Supermarkets.

I have a thing for the Supermarket
it's a form of meditation
nothing in here
reminds me of *my* life
I can do this...
I'm a spiritual giant
in the frozen food section
I'm Gandhi
in the Greeting Card section
and I'm Mother Teresa
in the check-out line
forgiving all the tabloid sinners
and connecting with something

greater than all of this.

"Credit or debit?

Paper or plastic?"

"Peace... please?"

I'd like

to give it a chance

after all,

it is the Holidays.

Beautiful Downtown Burbank

Car alarms,

big-screen TVs

and the passing traffic

heading to Hollywood

from the San Fernando Valley

lulls me to sleep at night

through walls

that were made

for transistor radios

and not for all this.

Walls that were made for

transient Lockheed workers

actors and bit players

from Warner Brothers Studios

who fell asleep at night

not to the sounds of technology

but to the sound of

the Johnny Carson Show

faintly in the background.

Through walls

that were made

for another time

and another volume.

To me, Burbank

has always felt

like Hollywood's backlot

It's where the first

talking picture was made

in the 1920s

and where a lot of stars lived

to get away from Hollywood.

I once saw Bob Hope

at the grocery store

...in Beautiful Downtown Burbank.

He was with his nurse.

The clerks told me he comes in

a few times a week

to walk laps

through the aisles,

it's his form of exercise.

I managed

in an *I Love Lucy*

type of way

to bump into him

in the stationery aisle

and without thinking

I grabbed a note pad

ripped a pen

out of its container

just in time

as he turned

the corner

arm in arm

with his nurse.

I asked her

if it would be okay

if I got his autograph.

She asked,

and he agreed

and asked me

my name.

"Iris" I said eagerly

and he sweetly replied,

"Okay Alice"

and scribbled

on my note pad

just that:

"To Alice, from Bob Hope,"

and shuffled off

singing Road to Morocco

as if he were still

on a movie set.

Even though

Burbank isn't

the *Mayberry-esque* place

it once was

when Johnny Carson's

Tonight Show

was on

five nights a week

and Bob Hope

spent his last days

doing laps

at Vons Grocery store

arm in arm with his nurse

instead of entertaining

at the USOs.

It's that bittersweet reminder

that nothing stays the same

and we do eventually grow old

even in TV Land.

Garbage Queen

She lives underneath me
and I can hear her
and her alcoholism
even when she's not
breaking things
fighting with her
loser boyfriend
trying to kill herself
remodeling at
4 in the morning
or throwing couches
at all hours of the night.

I can hear
her insanity
her pain
and her sorrow.

I can feel her hurt
and her anger through the floorboards
it's all she has left.
Somehow, she managed

in a drunken stupor
to flush a whole t-shirt
down the toilet.
It ended up
costing the Landlord
1200 dollars.
He was not happy
about this.
He sent her a letter
asking her
to respect
the neighbors
and to be careful
with her plumbing
and gas appliances
because the rest
of the building
was worried
that she would blow
the place up,
accidentally of course.
She calmed down
a lot after the Landlord
sent that letter.

She's afraid.

She's afraid that

everyone knows,

and they do.

She's angry

and thinks that

it's everyone else's fault.

I can tell by the way

she runs her garbage disposal.

She runs it long and often

she runs it empty and angry

it's her only weapon

it's all she has left.

She just runs that thing

for minutes

sometimes

half an hour

at a time.

It's like

Tourette

ventriloquism.

Her lips aren't moving

but the garbage disposal

says it all for her

spewing

her grinding anger.

It's her way

of showing

us all

as she's

backed into

a tiny corner

of her kitchen

with only a bottle

and a switch

and an angry hole.

Too bad she can't dispose

her own personal garbage

down that hole

too bad.

That Perfect Leopard Coat

I was six

when my mother

bought me

my first

leopard coat

it was the first

of many.

And it was perfect.

It fell right below the knees

and the collar

turned up

just right

landing mid-way

between

my ears

and neck

so, it looked like

it just happened

that way

naturally

and not like

I was trying

too hard

because if you're trying,

then you lose it

I took to

dragging my Leopard

after overhearing

two women talking
in the Ladies Room
at some fancy restaurant
in Chinatown.

I was workin' on
my 3rd Shirley Temple
getting a nice sugar buzz
when I overheard
one woman
tell the other,
"If you drag your fur
it looks like
you don't care
because it's just
'this old thing'
and considered
a sign of glamour."

So, I took to dragging *my fur*.
I'd slip on
my mother's
high heels
sun glasses

and neatly tuck

one of her

clutch purses

under my arm

wave around

an empty

cigarette holder

like Bette Davis.

And I'd saunter

around the house

all day long

dragging that Leopard

that perfect Leopard.

God how that coat

made me feel right

with the world.

A world

that was going crazy

it had just gone

from Black and White

to color

Transistor to Stereo

my brother

had just been drafted

into the Vietnam War

and we were

the only house

on the block

with a Color TV

and divorced parents.

Marilyn Monroe

was dead

and the cause of death

was just as much a mystery

as the assassination of JFK

and the world

was still riveting

from the aftershock…

Cause of death

for Marilyn and JFK

have never been confirmed

but I have a pretty good idea.

And as for the coat

my mother

gave it away

with all my Barbie Dolls

stuffed animals

and Dr. Seuss collection

high on Pharmaceutical speed

while "cleaning house"

at 3 in the morning.

There are some things

that change our lives,

and there are some things

that save our lives...

and even though

that was a long time ago

another Century

and another era

I've never stopped thinking

about that Leopard coat

or about how Marilyn Monroe and JFK,

along with the rest of the world

never saw it coming.

And how our lives

were never the same.

I lost my first tooth

The sun was shining

and the palm trees

were stretching and glistening

from Los Feliz to Franklin

all the way down

Vermont Avenue

we took a right on Franklin

to the Cedars of Lebanon Hospital

where a Scientology building

now sits.

My Grandma

lived right across the street

all her friends back in

Harlem and Brooklyn

were envious

because she moved to Hollywood

moved to an old building

that smelled of

cigarettes and sadness

with no Hollywood glamour

that I could see at all

with musty dark hallways

and a clankity old elevator.

That elevator scared me

I'd just seen the movie, "Hotel"

where the elevator plummets

to the ground and kills

everyone inside it.

And because of that

I hated my grandmother's elevator

and I always took the stairs

and my brothers

always made fun of me.

She was sick that day

and staying at the hospital

my mother had me wait

in the lobby while she went

to visit my grandmother

in her sick bed

I waited in that lobby alone

and when my tooth

came out

it just snapped

right off

in a most unnatural way

blood came pouring out

and I felt sick

sick because

I was alone

with no one to tell me

it was going to be alright...

sick because

I was alone

in a hospital

where they tended

to people

who were

bleeding all the time

couldn't anyone see

that I was bleeding?!

Even at the young age of 5

I could see the irony in all of this.

Tuesdays on Fairfax...

Every Tuesday
rain or shine
we'd go
to Canter's

and sit in one of those
big round booths
in the main
dining room
in the very back
so we could see
the whole restaurant
at a glance.

And she'd tell me stories
about my dad
and how he worked there
back in the 1950s
when he moved
the whole family
out to sunny California
from the East Coast
and stories
about my brothers,
all before I was born.
And we'd laugh
till we cried.

And then
we'd go over
to Farmer's Market
on 3rd & Fairfax
and sit outside
drinking cappuccinos
every Tuesday
rain or shine...

and we didn't even care
that we got wet
we were too busy
laughing.

How to Outrun the Slow Death of Your Mom

Stop sleeping
stay awake
stay distracted
or sleep too much
never get out of bed
stay in your pajamas
watch bad TV
watch good TV
watch old movies
watch anything
that has
nothing to do
with your life.

Do whatever
it takes
to not feel
chain smoke
do too much
for other people
people who didn't
ask for your help
and when they don't
appreciate you
get really mad at them
for not being psychic
about how
you've helped them.

———

Don't pay attention
to serious conversations
that have
anything to do
with your
dying mom.

Take on
as many projects
as possible
paint the kitchen floor
clean out
your closet
but don't throw
anything away
especially
the useless stuff
like phone numbers
on napkins
from people
you don't
remember
meeting.

Make plans
but don't
keep them
don't return
phone calls
especially
if they want

to talk about
your dying mom
no one
really wants
to hear
about it
it's too close
to home
we all
have mothers
some dead
and some
still alive
we all die
and it makes
people
uncomfortable
they only ask
because they don't
want to seem
like they don't care
but they
will only
say things
that hurt
you more
they don't mean to
because most people
don't know
what you are
really going through.

84

Stop being serious
listen only
to people
who are drunk
and don't want
to talk about
your dying mom.

Get in fights
with people
you love
over little things
like the dishes
or the trash
don't talk to
family members
who bug you
or don't
celebrate you
the ones who
want to
tell you
how to
live your life,
because it's impossible
for them
to know
so, you won't listen
and it will only
bug them more
so just

avoid them
all together.

Change everything
about your life
move
get a new job
sign on dotted lines
but don't read
the fine print.
Look hours
for things
you know
you will
never find.
If you drink alcohol
drink more
but don't
drink and drive
one death
is enough
if you don't
drink alcohol
then eat
and eat badly
sugar, starch, salt
and eat a lot of it
and make sure
it's not good for you
candy for breakfast
dessert for dinner

eat anything
that can't outrun you
and doesn't taste
like cardboard.

Frequent See's Candy
so much
that you know each other
on a first name basis.
Live way beyond
your means
use all your credit cards
max them out
buy stuff
you don't need
and let your temper
get the best of you.
Cuss and say things
you normally wouldn't
let your lower self
run the show
cuss people out
in traffic
drive fast
and tell people off
tell your friends off
tell them
what you've really
been thinking
all these years
get it out

get it all out
because in the end
after all this blows over
this *is* the only time
most people
will give
you a pass...

I am the Bastard Child

I am not my mother's daughter
or for that matter
my father's, either.
I am the bastard child
of Jack Kerouac
Jack Daniels
and Jack Sprat.
I am the lost
illegitimate
love child
of the ages
and I suffer
at the altar of...
or something
close to it.
I've given up
on perfection
and whether you think
it's right or not.
I've given up
on all the whores

and all my heroes

living and dead,

and I apologize

beyond the solar systems

for holding them

to the job

of my demise

and my rescue.

I am not my mother's daughter

I am her sister

I am not even my father's daughter

I am his wife.

I am the bastard child

of all those who have gone before me

who loved too much

too little

or not at all

and were crippled by it.

Love Gets Buried

Love gets buried

under bad days

in the trash

that forgot

to be taken out

and that

one loose handle

on the kitchen

cupboard door

that

no one

ever

fucking

fixes.

Love gets buried

under bills

and no jobs

crumbling buildings

and terrorism.

Love gets buried

screaming and muffled

under the sound

of alcoholic neighbors

who always win

because they're drunk

and louder.

Love gets buried

and forgotten

under countless

unpaid parking tickets

lost souls for loved ones

and motel drug overdoses.

Love gets buried

under friends dying too soon

before they ever had the chance

of a fully realized life.

Love gets buried

under the heartless

shuffle of HMOs

finding things

that aren't there

and not treating
things that are.

Love gets buried
under lost blood tests
and bad carpet.

Love gets buried
and sometimes
love resurrects
and sometimes
love just gets buried.

You're Like a Burning Building

(For Danny D.)

…and it doesn't matter

that you made me so crazy

it doesn't matter

that you are certifiably crazy.

I think about your arms

and how the life force

pulses through your veins

and how I could build

a whole world

around your forearms.

And the lines in your face

how beautiful you are

even as you are aging.

You can tell that you were

drop dead gorgeous

at one time

and that women and men

threw themselves at you

even if you *were*

an asshole

because you had the whole world

eating out of the palms of your hands

as you stepped on their toes.

And how you could always

make me laugh the kind of laugh

that can't be stopped

that comes back

hours and days later

when I'd think about it

and how you always

brought me flowers

and gifts for no reason,

just to make me happy

but you'd always say

"Now remember this

for when you hate me."

And how being with you

was one of the most

exciting rides

I'd ever been on

even on the scary parts

when I thought

for sure you'd burn

the house down.

Or when

I had to visit you in jail

and how seeing you

in prison blues

behind bullet proof glass

made it all make sense,

It was a good look for you…

And how you could always

bring it out of me

and get me

or anyone

to do things

we never imagined

or thought of.

We were all

your puppets

weren't we?

You'd call at three

and four and five

in the morning

after being up

for days on end

<u>on</u> yet *another* one

of your speed runs.
And every time
you would talk about
how you just
want to stop
and this time
you will.
Or what about
the time
we sang
Crosby, Stills, Nash and Young
in your air-conditioned car
in hot, stacked traffic
and purposely
way off key
"I am yours
you are mine
you are what you are
and you make it haaaaaard."
and you do
make it so hard.
Yes,
you're like a burning building
that I have to run from

but I want the burning building

to want me to stay

but you would never admit that

and what good would it do if you did

in order to stay

I'd have to put that fire out

and we both know

that's not possible.

Yes, you make it hard

you're like a burning building.

But what a lovely way to burn....

Paper Hearts

Sometimes
I picture
a different
kind of life
for us.
Free and simple
where dreams

are still in the lead

and financial fear

isn't winning.

The fear of mortality

hasn't set in

and we're in a setting

in the middle of nowhere

that takes on

a kind of 1970s

noir sensibility

and values.

A time before

we hadn't hurt

or unintentionally

betrayed each other

and broke promises

because someone else

had a better deal

that lasts only as long

as 4 am conversations do,

as we were just trying

to figure it all out.

we had no past

and our future

was still bright

seamless and

filled with hope.

But fear of intimacy

comes in so many

different forms

and so does

fear of rejection

throw in some

unintentional neglect

and you have

the perfect destination

where love

goes to die.

It's a brutal tragedy

with a cliché ending

I do hope you find

whatever it is

you're looking for

lost out there

in your own private

John Huston film.

And this time

with a much

happier ending.

Punk Rock Royalty

(For Ratsass)

SOMEWHERE IN SACRAMENTO CALIFORNIA

AT SOME WELL-KNOWN CRASH PAD

SOMETIME IN THE MIDDLE OF THE WEEK

AND SOMETIME IN THE MIDDLE

OF THE AFTERNOON

DAY AND TIME

CUSTOMARILY UNKNOWN

TO RESIDENTS OF HOUSE

THE DISHES HAVEN'T BEEN WASHED

SINCE JULY (AND IT'S SEPTEMBER)

HALF EMPTY TO GO BOXES

WITH TWO-WEEK OLD PIZZA

AND TACO BELL REMAINS

99 CENT BURGERS

 FROM AM/PM

AND EMPTY BOTTLES

OF PLAIN WRAP LIQUOR

AND BEER CANS

LAY STREWN ACROSS THE KITCHEN FLOOR

LEAVING NOT EVEN A TRAIL

IN THE LIVING ROOM

THERE'S 4 GUYS

WHO HAVEN'T SLEPT

IN 3 DAYS

TRYING TO PUMP LIFE

OUT OF A KEG THAT'S

BEEN FINISHED SINCE THE WEEKEND

AND 2 PIT BULLS

GNAWING ON OLD RIB BONES

THERE'S FLIES EVERYWHERE

AND IT'S HOT

THE HICKOIDS

TALES OF TERROR

FANG

AND JOHNNY THUNDERS

IS BLARING OUT OF BEER SOAKED SPEAKERS

THAT PERIODICALLY

KEEP SHORTING OUT

THE TV IS ON

BUT THE SOUND IS OFF

SHOWING "BLUE VELVET"

FOR THE 5TH TIME THAT DAY

(MUST BE ANOTHER "FRANK" FEST)

AND IN THE MIDDLE OF ALL OF THIS

YOU'RE LOCKED AWAY

IN THE BATHROOM

LIKE PUNK ROCK ROYALTY

SITTIING ON YOUR THRONE

JACKING-OFF TO MY PICTURE

IN "FLIPSIDE" MAGAZINE

FOR THE SECOND TIME THAT DAY

THANK YOU,

I FEEL HONORED.

White Chick from Pacoima

An R&B station
plays in the distance
in perfect rhythm
with the washers and dryers.

The stripper
methodically folds laundry
while her wordless boyfriend
sits watching
with a glazed look
on his face
as if he'd done
one too many Xanax
along with a thousand
other things
trying to shut off his brain.
Their chihuahua *Tyson*
keeps licking my toes
as I fold *my* laundry.
It's 3 in the afternoon
the air is hot and still

———

in the laundromat.

As I look around
the muscle guys joke
and check out girls.
Hispanic women
with their babies
doing the laundry
for their whole family.
Middle aged women
in glasses
with wide asses
work at not making
eye contact.
A 40 something
mentally challenged son
folds his laundry
with the help
of his
70 something mother.

We are all
regulars here
regulars who never speak

we just come

and do our laundry.

This small but

common bond.

And for a moment in time

I can't imagine

wanting to be

anywhere else.

Epilogue

Tales from the Tropicana Motel

(Reprinted from Slake Quarterly, 2010)

The Tropicana Motel was known worldwide during its heyday. 8585 Santa Monica Boulevard was a haven and hideout for actors, artists, writers, poets, directors, sports figures, music producers, film producers, and rock stars. Just a limo ride or drunken, one-cigarette stumble down La Cienega from the Sunset Strip. It was Chelsea Hotel with poolside and AstroTurf. Parties sometimes lasted for months and often ended in mayhem. There was a constant parade of groupies, photographers, and drug dealers.

Word on the street was that anything you desired-- no matter how bizarre, sleazy, or unsavory--could be had at the Trop, and for an extremely low nightly rate. All just a stone's throw away from the West Hollywood Sheriff's station.

In the 1950s, the motel was a getaway for the Hollywood's better-known character actors. But as Hollywood changed, so did the ownership. In 1963 the motel was sold to its fourth owner, soon-to-be Hall of Famer Sandy Koufax, strikeout artist of the Los Angeles Dodgers. Being a smart businessman, he immediately changed the sign to read, "Sandy Koufax's Tropicana Motel," which brought a whole new clientele. The culture shifted to television stars and rock gods. From 1963 onward the Trop functioned as a boho playground, pioneered by Jim Morrison of the Doors, who hung around the Palms, a low-rent (and nearly as infamous) dyke bar across the street from the Tropicana. He would drink there all night before stumbling across the street to pass out. Mornings after, he'd write many of the songs that became hits for the Doors. Waves of other musicians followed. The motel was also the site of numerous photo sessions and legendary band interviews, and it served as the location for the Andy Warhol films, *Heat* and *Trash*. The party kept going until 1988, when the building was razed and replaced with a Ramada Inn.

Duke's Coffee Shop, underneath the Tropicana, served copious amounts of good, inexpensive food to poor artists and musicians as well as record and film execs. The seating was family style, which meant tourists from the mid-west could be eating breakfast next to Mohammad Ali or Clash front man Joe Strummer.

The rooms at the Tropicana looked like Little Richard decorated them with somebody's midwestern grandma on a lost weekend. There were a few private bungalows at the back of the property where Tom Waits and Chuck E. Weiss, among others took up long-term residence. The kidney-bean-shaped pool was surrounded by AstroTurf and painted black, to hide the rust stains from patio furniture that was regularly tossed in the water. Regulars knew better than to dive into the pool--you might have an underwater rendezvous with a chaise lounge, or, worse, a syringe or two. Under the Trop's junglelike foliage there were orgies, murders, suicides, ODs, love triangles, marriages, and drunken brawls on a daily basis. There were even a number of struggling bands living in their cars in the Trop's back parking lot. (which the management was fully aware of).

It was not unlikely to see Iggy and the Stooges, Janis Joplin, Van Morrison, the Beach Boys, Led Zeppelin,

Frank Zappa, Bruce Springsteen, Eddie Cochran, Elvis Costello, Nick Lowe, Blondie, The Cramps, Johnny Thunders and the Heartbreakers, the Damned, the Clash, the Dead Boys, Johnny Cash, Dennis Hopper, Evel Knievel, Sam Shepard, Levi and the Rockats, Legendary photographer Leee Black Childers, Marianne Faithfull, William Burroughs, Nico, Lou Reed and the rest of the Velvet Underground, the New York Dolls, the Ramones, and locals like the Runaways, Rodney Bingenheimer, Van Halen, Guns N Roses, the Germs, and the Red Hot Chili Peppers wandering the halls eating at Duke's or lounging by the pool.

When the Tropicana Motel's escapades came to a grinding halt in 1988 after three decades, it marked the end of an era...or two or three. It had stood as bacchanalia central in the time before AIDS and MTV, demographics and gentrification. While it lasted though, the Trop was ground zero for some of the best times that the underbelly of Los Angeles ever saw.

The End

About The Author

Iris Berry is a native Angelino and one of the true and original progenitors of the L.A. punk scene. She is the author of several books including *Two Blocks East of Vine, The Daughters of Bastards, The Underground Guide to Los Angeles* and *All That Shines Under the Hollywood Sign.* Internationally known, her wit and often dark, factual accuracy and empathy for her subjects has brought her critical acclaim as well as a huge fan base. She writes her experiences with grace and deadly precision. Her lullaby-and bedtime-story voice is like a haunting tour of Los Angeles that lingers like one of the city's unsolved murders.

Berry has appeared in numerous films, TV commercials, documentaries, and iconic rock videos. In the 1980s she was a singer for the punk band the Lame Flames. Later Berry co-founded and toured extensively with her band The Ringling Sisters, who recorded with legendary producer Lou Adler (A&M Records). Berry also sang and wrote songs and recorded with the Dickies, the Flesh Eaters and Pink Sabbath. She's received two certificates of merit from the city of Los Angeles for her contribution as a Los Angeles writer/historian and for her extensive charity work. From 2010-2014 she was on the Board of Directors for Beyond Baroque Literary/Arts Center. Iris is the co-founder, editor and publisher for her imprint PUNK HOSTAGE PRESS where continues to champion for original voices.

About The Illustrator

Scott Aicher's love for art began at the early age of five when he won 3 blue ribbons after his mother entered his paintings in a local art show. Largely a self-taught artist, he has had many years of experience as a professional artist starting in humble print shops, then later advancing to illustration for entertainment, record and surf companies. Scott's work can be seen on various flyers and record covers for: Bad Religion, Pennywise, Firehose, Chemical People, Jeff Dahl, Rikk Agnew, TSOL, the Angry Samoans, Chicano Batman, Mike Watt, Toys That Kill, Rolling Blackouts, Love Canal, Blood on the Saddle, Left Insane and Nip Drivers to name a few. Along with illustrating two books by TSOL front man Jack Grisham, *Untamed* and *Code Blue* (Punk Hostage Press). And Iris Berry's *All That Shines Under the Hollywood Sign* and *The Trouble with Palm Trees* (Punk Hostage Press).

Growing up in Southern California provided much of the outlandish cartoon style that breathes throughout his work. Often playful with a bright bold color pallet his work falls mainly in the Pop Surreal or Kustom Culture genres. He collects Toys, Vinyl Records, Comics, Art Books and Guitars. He and his family moved to Texas. They love the open space and wildlife there and especially the southern hospitality. It's rough finding a good Pizza, but he's enjoying the pimento cheese sandwiches.

Danny Baker
> *Fractured* - 2012

A Razor
> *Better Than a Gun in A Knife* Fight - 2012
> *Drawn Blood: Collected Works*
> *From D.B.P.LTD., 1985-1995* - 2012
> *Beaten Up Beaten Down* - 2012
> *Small Catastrophes in A Big World* - 2012
> *Half- Century Status* - 2013
> *Days of Xmas Poems* - 2014
> *Puro Purismo* – 2021

Iris Berry
> *The Daughters of Bastards* - 2012
> *All That Shines Under the Hollywood Sign* – 2019
> *The Trouble with Palm Trees* - 2021

C.V. Auchterlonie
> *Impress* - 2012

Yvonne De la Vega
> *Tomorrow, Yvonne - Poetry & Prose for Suicidal Egoists* - 2012

Carolyn Srygley- Moore
> *Miracles Of the Blog: A Series* - 2012

Rich Ferguson
> *8th & Agony* -2012

Jack Grisham
> *Untamed* -2013
> *Code Blue: A Love Story* ~ 2014
> *Pulse of the World. Arthur Chance, Punk Rock Detective* - 2021

Dennis Cruz
> *Moth Wing Tea* - 2013
> *The Beast Is We* - 2018

Frank Reardon
> *Blood Music* - 2013

Pleasant Gehman
> *Showgirl Confidential* – 2013
> *Rock 'n' Roll Witch – A Memoir of Sex Magick, Drugs and Rock 'n'*
> *Roll* - 2022

Hollie Hardy
> *How To Take a Bullet and Other Survival Poems* – 2014

Joel Landmine
> *Yeah, Well...* – 2014
> *Things Change* - 2021

More Books on Punk Hostage Press

A.D. Winans
>Dead Lions – 2014

S.A. Griffin
>*Dreams Gone Mad with Hope* - 2014

SB Stokes
>*History Of Broken Love Things* – 2014

Nadia Bruce- Rawlings
>*Scars* - 2014
>*Driving in The Rain* - 2020

Lee Quarnstrom
>*WHEN I WAS A DYNAMITER, Or, how a Nice Catholic Boy Became a Merry Prankster, a Pornographer, and a Bridegroom Seven Times* - 2014

Alexandra Naughton
>*I Will Always Be Your Whore/Love Songs for Billy Corgan* - 2014
>*You Could Never Objectify Me More Than I've Already Objectified Myself* -2015

Michele McDannold
>*Stealing The Midnight from A Handful of Days* – 2014

Maisha Z Johnson
>*No Parachutes to Carry Me Home* - 2015

Michael Marcus
>*#1 Son and Other Stories* - 2017

Danny Garcia
>*LOOKING FOR JOHNNY, The Legend of Johnny Thunders* - 2018

William S. Hayes
>*Burden of Concrete* - 2020

Todd Moore
>*Dillinger's Thompson* - 2020

Dan Denton
>*$100-A-Week Motel* - 2021

Jack Henry
>Driving W/ Crazy, living with madness – 2021

Joe Donnelly
>*So Cal, Dispatches From the End of the World* - 2022

Patrick O'Neil
>*Anarchy at the Circle K – On the Road with Dead   Kennedys, TSOL, Flipper, Subhumans…and Heroin* – 2022